"Once again Dwight Lee Wolter offers us an insightful and compassionate look at the legacy of the dysfunctional family. In his newest book, *Forgiving Our Parents,* we are led through his honest and gut-wrenching process of understanding and forgiving his parents. As we experience his personal story, we learn much about ourselves along the way."

> Patricia O'Gorman, Ph.D.,
> Philip Oliver-Diaz, M.S.W.,
> authors of *Breaking the Cycle of Addiction*
> and *12 Steps to Self-Parenting*

"In part, we learn to forgive by remembering not to forget. Leading us through the thickets of forgiveness, Dwight Lee Wolter strikes a remarkable balance between toughness and compassion, anger and empathy. One further bonus—his prose is almost unforgivably good!"

> F. Forrester Church, Ph.D., minister,
> Unitarian Church of All Souls, New York;
> *New York Post* columnist;
> author of *Everyday Miracles: Stories from Life*

Forgiving Our Parents

For Adult Children from Dysfunctional Families

Dwight Lee Wolter

CompCare® Publishers

Minneapolis, Minnesota

©1989 by Dwight Lee Wolter
All rights reserved.
Published in the United States
by CompCare Publishers.

Library of Congress Cataloging-in-Publication Data

Wolter, Dwight Lee.
    Forgiving our parents
    1. Adult child abuse victims—Mental health. 2. Adult chil-
dren of alcoholics—Mental health 3. Forgiveness 4. Problem
families. I. Title
RC569.5.C55W55 1989   616.85'822   89-1030
ISBN 0-89638-189-7

Cover design by Jeremy Gale
Interior design by MacLean and Tuminelly

Inquiries, orders, and catalog requests should be
addressed to:
CompCare Publishers
2415 Annapolis Lane
Minneapolis, MN 55441
Call toll free 800/328-3330
(Minnesota residents, 612/559-4800)

5   4   3   2
93   92   91   90   89

This book is dedicated to the memory of
John Lennon. It was he who gave me the courage
to be so open about my past and so hopeful
about my future.

Contents

Preface

I was almost asleep when I heard my bedroom door creak open and a sliver of light stretched across my face. I lay still and pretended I was not awake.

My father sneaked into my room. He knelt beside my bed. I felt him staring at me. I heard his heavy breathing. I smelled beer and brandy on his breath and in the pores of his skin. He gently ran his fingers through my hair and patted me on the head a few times. He touched my shoulder very, very lightly—the way a person might sneak the touch of a painting in a museum while the guard isn't looking. He leaned over the edge of the bed and kissed me once on the forehead. Then he did...nothing. I could feel him staring at me again. He slowly stood up and sneaked back out of my room. I heard the door creak closed as the seam of light retracted across my face.

My father was a mean and violent man. Yet when he came into my room to kiss me good-night—an act he could never do when I was awake—I knew he loved me.

This was the best he could offer. I felt sorry for him. I was an eleven-year-old boy who felt sorry for his father. I saw how pathetic he was. He was killing me slowly, but I felt sorry for him. He was killing me because he loved me. He was so unable to accept love, he was so unable to accept himself, that he had to kill all traces of love, and all traces of himself which he found in his children.

I think my father felt sorry for me because I had to be his son. He knew I was a good boy. He knew I had done no wrong. He knew I was suffering at his hands. He knew he could not stop abusing me. My father also felt sorry for himself. He knew he and his son would never know each other, just like my father and his father never knew each other. The cycle of abuse was familiar to him, but he was powerless to stop it.

I know all this, now that I am an adult and have been working on my feelings about my parents. But as a child all I knew was that something was terribly wrong.

When my father left my room, I stared at the wall and tried to stuff my feelings deep within me, out of his reach. He had showed love to me. But it was too late. I was only eleven years old, but it had already been years since I had made a vow to myself that I would never show or feel love for him again. I had killed my capacity to love before he could get to me, so that by the time he reached me, I was already emotionally dead.

I wondered how I was feeling, if I was sad that my father was my enemy. I wondered if he knew I was awake all along, and his loving gestures were merely a hoax designed to coax me into trusting him so he could violate my trust once again. As numbness and sleep overcame me and I closed my dry eyes against the night, I wondered if I would ever feel again.

Who Forgives Whom?

When I was a little boy I forgot to take my dog for a walk. He made a mess on the living room floor, so my father shot and killed him. Thirty years later I am writing this book and exploring the possibility of forgiving my father for what some people consider to be unforgivable behavior. Some think I am crazy for even thinking about forgiving him. Others think it is a noble and wonderful thing I am attempting to do. I don't know how I feel about it. I want to remain as open as I can during this journey into the consideration of forgiving our parents.

Everyone was raised by someone, and there are issues involving forgiveness in all families. Perhaps your parents had—or still have—problems with alcohol or other substances. Maybe they never drank at all, but were physically or emotionally abusive. Perhaps your parents died and you still carry with you an uncomfortable anger or sadness at being abandoned by them. Perhaps your parents are living but you have little or no contact with them. Perhaps you see no need to forgive *them*, and only wish that they would forgive *you*.

Perhaps you weren't raised by your parents and your issues of forgiveness are with other relatives or foster parents. Who knows? Maybe it's your father-in-law you have a difficult time forgiving!

Perhaps your forgiveness issues have shifted their focus from you and your parents to you and your children. Have your children done something which you consider unforgivable? Or do your children feel unable to forgive *you*?

No matter what your situation, the absence of a nurturing relationship with your parents, your loved ones, and yourself is the central theme here. The object of this book is not to have you read it and then immediately call your parents to forgive them. This book is an *exploration* into forgiveness. It demands no immediate action. Forgiveness is a choice only you can make.

A Try at Forgiveness

In early recovery from substance abuse I called my parents and begged them to forgive me for being such a bad son.

You see, my father had once had such high hopes for me. I had let him down terribly. All of his other children failed to make a great impression on the world. And I, as the youngest child, the last hope, had also fallen into the muck of mediocrity. Not only had I failed to achieve the greatness my parents had prophesied for me to all their friends throughout my entire life—I hadn't come close to being even average or normal. I wasn't coping well with life, to say the least. I felt that I had disgraced myself and my parents' good name.

But since I was in recovery, perhaps I had one last stab at greatness left in me after all! I would be an immense success and buy my parents a little house with a picket fence and a pool and a private nurse for them to order around; that would surely pay them back for all the suffering I had caused them. I would start a huge company that manufactured who-knows-what, and I would hire all my siblings and thus snatch them too from the clutches of mediocrity. And they would be very grateful to me, and, of course, to God! They would toast me each night at their family dinner table with long-stemmed glasses filled with sparkling apple cider. (They would have long since given up drinking, because who needs to escape when life is so good, thanks to Dwight!) I would be like Tiny Tim in Charles Dickens' *A Christmas Carol*, the crippled catalyst for change. (Like Tiny Tim, I was crippled as a child.) Because of my suffering and indomitable spirit, the family would be saved. I would be the Family Hero.

My father heard my petition with the benevolence of a priest receiving confession. But then it slipped out that I didn't feel he was the easiest person to reveal myself to. I began to squirm as I told him this because I had always assumed that the communication problems were rooted in *me*. All through my life if I ever implied that even a speck of responsibility might lie with my father, his expression would change. His eyes would narrow and his pupils would dilate. He would lift his chin to give the impression that he was looking down on me, even though I am taller than he is.

Now, on the telephone, he said, in a voice elevated by strength and the knowledge of my unseen discomfort, "...it seems that all my children are hiding from something."

"I'm not hiding from anybody," I said in a voice filled with self-doubt. My mind was flipping through the computer of past experience, searching frantically for evidence to support his conclusion, since I believed that Daddy would have no reason to say such a thing to his son unless it were true.

We talked for a while longer on the phone with me probing, trying to decipher the strange code my father has always talked in. My father offered no help. It reminded me of how he always seemed to enjoy making people dig for meaning in his vagaries. I felt I should have a dictionary handy whenever I spoke with him because he would use such huge words and obscure references. But a dictionary never could help me understand his bizarre thoughts and subtle put-downs. I would scratch my head and either confess to or hide my confusion. He would sit back, apparently content in his belief that the only thing that stood between him and being understood was the lesser intelligence of the person he was speaking to.

We ended our telephone conversation with my feeling that my father was, as usual, somehow right and I was, as usual, somehow wrong. Off the phone, unconnected by time or distance or Ma Bell, my true feelings began to emerge.

I felt that same fear of vulnerability I knew long ago when my father sneaked into my room. The feeling was that if I opened my heart to my parents—if I revealed even the slightest gleam of humanity, if I lowered my cannons and gave my personal army the day off, if I showed an emotion other than fear or rage, if they had the slightest clue that I was emotionally alive—they would attack me. Being vulnerable was dangerous.

I began to feel that my parents owed *me* an apology for the way they treated me. This feeling was a long time coming. I had never before I realized that I had rights they chronically violated. I assume that people usually afford one another a certain level of respect and decency; this seemed to me to be absolutely missing in my family. I remember envying my neighbor's dog, which my parents would pat on the head and coo nice things to.

As these memories began to surface, I waited for my parents to ask for *my* forgiveness. This, I felt, they certainly owed me, especially since I had already asked them to forgive me. Now it was their turn. Not a word did they speak. This made my blood boil.

Time and Timing

I realized I had been too eager to forgive. I had jumped right into forgiveness as soon as I recognized the abuse that had taken place. I thought I was being a wonderful person by forgiving my parents right away. But what I was really trying to do was to go from zero to ten in a single bound.

I was trying to avoid the work, pain, and anger of becoming aware of what had happened to me as a child. I didn't want to relive the panic of being a child in that house, or to set foot in the hot river of rage that flowed between my parents and me. I didn't want to feel my powerlessness over my parents' tantrums and my inability to escape them. I found it painful to think about how intimate relationships were very difficult for me, in part because of the abuse I suffered in my family of origin. I didn't want to admit how hard it is to be a good father to my daughter because I had learned virtually no healthy ways to bring up a child. I wanted nothing to do with any of this past pain. I just wanted to forgive my parents and get it over with.

I have not always been so squeamish about dealing with my parents. As a child I was very willing to forgive. I was eager to listen and to understand. I wanted to help. My father would come home from work with a tornado under one arm and a hurricane under the other. Then he would proceed to blow the place apart. In the calm after the storm we would make jokes and be extra kind. Our family was like the crew at the Indianapolis 500 auto race. We would descend on my father to assess the damage, to locate the cause of the overheating, to replace the broken parts, and to give him something to drink. We wanted so desperately to forgive. He appeared as shaken and confused about the abuse as we were. We wanted to lift his obvious guilt. We wanted to love.

He abused us and we forgave and forgave and forgave. Like a bronze statue of someone that no one ever heard of, he would sit, sullen and guilty, his face washed blue by the light of the television he wasn't really watching. He accepted our gifts of love and attention and forgiveness and he offered nothing in return but an empty glass, which was our job to fill.

It took some years, but eventually our family fell apart. Not all families do. Some families, in the midst of crisis, pull together in order to survive. Floods in the spring, earthquakes in California, the New York City blackout—all these are famous for the sense of community and camaraderie that they can inspire. But these same adversities also produce looters and vultures. In the face of adversity my family fell into chaos. The pain tore us apart.

In my parents' home I saw my siblings disintegrate. Like steam from a kettle, they once were hot and strong. But they soon dissipated into the air. I have not seen or talked to them in many years.

Today I realize that, just as it took time to get into this difficult situation, it will take time to get out of it. In addition to time, it will take good timing. Knowing when I am ready to offer forgiveness, when to pick up the phone or write the letter, when to leave someone alone who seems to have absolutely no interest in what I'm bothered by—all this takes time and timing. There is no time limit, no bell that will ring to tell us when to put down our pencils. There is no pressure on us to forgive, except that which we place on ourselves.

Seeing Clearly

Before we can make a decision to forgive our parents, we must take a clear and close look at what we are attempting to forgive. Before we eat, we want to know what we are eating. Before we sign, we want to know what we are signing. Before we forgive, we need to know what it is we are forgiving. We must look at what happened and review the damage done, even though it is painful to do so.

Forgiveness is not amnesia. It is not a drug we take to forget the pain. Dismissing the past as over and done with—and therefore not relevant to life today—is not going to make the problem go away. We need to remember *what* we are forgiving, as well as understand when to forgive and why.

When we decide to investigate our relationship with our parents, intense feelings trapped inside us since childhood may come flying out. It may feel like a root canal without novocain. These ancient feelings can be frightening—especially rage or hatred.

We may be tempted to call ourselves names such as "stupid," "bad," "self-pitying," or "ungrateful."

Judging our feelings will only make the process more difficult. There is no such thing as "bad" feelings, only comfortable or uncomfortable ones. Not judging our feelings as bad or good allows us to feel safer when uncomfortable feelings surface. It is important to let these feelings come to the top so we can see the deep-seated issues we are dealing with.

It seems that certain feelings are valued more highly than others. Love is valued more highly than hate, for example, and this makes sense. Clichés—like "forgive and forget" or "to err is human, to forgive divine"—reinforce these favored feelings. But adult children from dysfunctional homes may use these cliches to feel guilty about their inability or unwillingness to forgive. It is a sound idea to focus on our *own* emerging feelings about forgiveness rather than relying on familial or societal dictates. Well-intentioned cliches should not be mistaken for truths.

Clichés and slogans are intended as easy-to-remember summations of knowledge and wisdom, but they can be misused. Unfortunately, they are sometimes used to silence people or to deny feelings. When adult children from dysfunctional homes are reliving their childhood traumas in an attempt to get at the root of the problems, they might be told: "Don't analyze—utilize." One positive intention of this slogan is to encourage the person not to dwell on or intellectualize the problem to the point of inability to act. But the slogan is often used to encourage people to *not think about* their traumatic past. That way, whoever hurled the slogans or clichés in the first place—sometimes a helping professional who may have come from an alcoholic or dysfunctional home—can remain in denial about his or her *own* past too, by stifling others' attempts to bring up old hurts like these.

We can choose to believe such slogans and feel bad about falling short of these ideal states, or we can choose to ignore them until we investigate forgiveness a little further.

We also have the right to rewrite these sayings to suit our own needs, or to have some fun while reminding ourselves that they are not written in stone, regardless of their familiarity or popularity. "To err is human, to forgive divine" could be rewritten as "to err is human, to forgive is optional." "Forgive and forget" could be rewritten as "forgive, but don't forget, or you may set yourself up to *keep on* forgiving and forgiving and forgiving."

Seeing Is Not Enough

Awareness of the problems we have with our parents and how we feel about them is the first step toward change. Forgiveness is near the end of a long process which begins with the simple decision to feel our feelings without judging them. But feelings of loss and pain do not simply go away by seeing that a problem exists. Staring at the problem won't change it either. First we see it, then we feel it, and then we sit with it. We acknowledge our painful feelings as being part of us. We might feel immense sadness and be tempted to run away from ourselves. We might even regret our willingness to look directly at the problem and admit our past was as bad as—or worse than—we thought it was.

One reason we might regret looking at the problem and then sitting with the feelings is that we lose the last vestige of hope that we will be able to make the family "right." It is painful to realize, but true nonetheless, that many of us still cling to our paintbrushes, years after the canvas has dried, waiting for an opportunity to change the picture. Looking at the picture, possibly with tears in our eyes—and accepting that what happened happened and cannot be undone—is not an opportunity most people jump at gleefully.

This is all extremely painful. But admission and acceptance of the unhealthy aspects of our relationship with our parents is essential before we can change the way we view our parents and ourselves. It takes insight and a lot of courage to pursue this process.

To Forgive or
Not to Forgive

 I remember one day as a child when my father knew my mother was coming home late. He waited for her by the picture window in the living room. When he saw her car approach he quickly turned off all the lights. He went into the kitchen and stuck his hands in the freezer. Then he hid behind the front door. When she entered the room he ran his ice cold hands up under her dress and grabbed her. He laughed and laughed and laughed. So did she, after a while. It was so nice to see father and mother in a good mood for a change.

I sometimes use these little episodes of humor and accidental encounters with fun as ways to feel connected to my parents. Not every moment of every day was terrible. There was occasional laughter, but it was *always at someone's expense.* I still use humor—as I did then—to deny how very difficult my childhood was. We laughed hard and we laughed whenever we could because we never knew when it would be our turn to be the brunt of someone's sadistic humor.

I choose to distinguish between forgiveness for things that happened merely because my parents are human and make mistakes—and forgiveness for things done out of maliciousness.

If our parents were poorly parented themselves and thus learned poor rules for parenting their own children, then it is truly the family system that can be labeled "bad," not the individuals in it. It's not surprising that people from dysfunctional homes tend to parent dysfunctionally. Abused children identify with their abusive parents and reenact the abuse with their own children, thus remaining loyal to family tradition. Abused children often grow up to be abusive parents. Intellectually at least, this explanation makes the abuse more understandable and less "blameworthy."

Besides the mistakes they make because they are human, or because they too grew up in dysfunctional families, some parents simply are not nice people.

Whatever was the cause of my parents' behavior, they plucked away at the self-esteem of their children, feather by feather, until we stood naked and defenseless in the world. The fact that my parents have problems, and that their problems may extend well beyond substance abuse, makes a difference in how I view them. But that is no reason to throw away my feelings, or to deny the weight of the bundles of wet hay my parents loaded on my back as I stumbled without direction down the difficult road that has led to where I stand today.

As I think about unforgivable behavior, I am reminded of two events in recent history. The first is the trial and conviction of a World War II criminal. He had committed terrible deeds and was judged guilty and sentenced to die. At the sentencing, the judge admonished the nation involved not to forgive. He told the courtroom and the world that a thousand deaths was not enough to do justice to the heinous crime this man had committed.

Here is the notion that to forgive is the same as to forget—to forgive is a betrayal of an entire country and people. While acknowledging that the convict was now an elderly, devoutly religious person living a simple family life that bore no resemblance to his horrid past, the court decision was the death penalty—not an act of revenge, according to the court, but an act of justice. In this case, they felt that justice was best served by a refusal to forgive.

The second "unforgivable" incident is the shooting of a religious leader by a fanatic. The religious leader, after his wounds were healed, paid a visit to the man in prison. He prayed for and forgave his assailant.

I draw no conclusion from these isolated, but somehow related, situations. Both of them seem to me to be equally bizarre and disturbing. I am as confused by the judgment of the court as I am by the religious leader's tolerance as I am by my own mixed feelings. I mention these incidences only to point out that there seems to be no socially sanctioned, correct, mature, morally perfect approach to forgiveness *or* nonforgiveness. The choice is truly up to us.

Part of me believes that my parents do not deserve to be forgiven. Sometimes the mere thought of them unlocks my vast warehouse of righteousness and indignation. Recently while riding on a bus I saw a parent on the street corner yelling at her child. That triggered the "start" button on the carrousel of horror, which is the memory of my youth. I searched frantically for the "stop" button, but it took a long, long time to put those memories out of my mind.

The predicament that a lot of adult children from dysfunctional homes find themselves in is that, because of the family investment in denying that a problem exists, so that they don't have to face a very painful reality, their parents cannot—or will not—take responsibility for their role in the relationship problems their children now face.

This parental abdication of responsibility, coupled with subtle cultural encouragement to "forgive and forget," creates a family rift for some adult children which they have trouble breaching. They want to forgive, but they also want their parents to own up to their part of the problem. When this does not happen, forgiveness is more difficult.

In fact, if parents' unwillingness or inability to accept responsibility is chronic, many adult children will become adamant in their refusal to forgive. It's like being tripped over every day in the same place by the same person, with never an accompanying apology or acknowledgment of what happened. The result is anger. Habitual abuse is hard to forgive.

I sometimes stomp my feet and repeat my childhood oath that I will go to my grave without forgiving my parents. But another part of me allows myself this memory of pain and helplessness. There is more to the story of why I am sometimes reluctant to forgive my parents than is evident by simply telling the tale of my difficult youth.

Everyone I have ever met and talked to about my childhood has understood why I have a hard time forgiving my parents. No one is surprised at my blame and anger. My life story is an airtight case of child abuse and neglect.

But why did I hold on so tight to this dysfunctional family for so long?

To Forgive Our Parents
Is to Face Ourselves

T he process of forgiveness might *begin* by looking at our parents, but it always *ends* by looking at ourselves. Forgiveness is more about *us* than it is about *them*.

Many of us who were raised in dysfunctional homes use *unforgiveness* and *resentment* as a means of keeping us away from our true feelings. By focusing on our parents' failings, we don't have to take a look at our own character defects. Rage, fear, and anger lurk within an unforgiving heart. Who wants to look at that? Many of us have had so much pain in childhood that, as adults, we avoid pain at any cost. By not looking at the issues we have with our parents, we remain locked within a familiar, often negative bias.

To forgive implies a willingness to admit that our old ways of dealing with our parents don't work anymore. We sense a need for change, but are unsure of how to go about it. After a lifetime of focusing on our parents, it might feel terribly selfish to consider our own welfare first. We may feel we will again open ourselves to the same abuse we were subjected to as children, and we may have sworn never to allow ourselves to be hurt that way again. But to forgive our parents doesn't mean we have to be their friend. We might not be able to interact with them at all. But we *can* interact with ourselves.

We stare at our parents until our eyes hurt. We probe their lives more than our own, because it might be much more painful to turn our eyes around and look into ourselves. We may claim that it's not that we aren't willing to forgive—but that they don't deserve it. Sometimes we might believe that they deserve to be forgiven. Sometimes we would still rather focus on what we believe our parents might be forgiven for, than on our own ability (or inability) to forgive.

Anger

In avoiding looking at ourselves, we also avoid our underlying feelings. We keep sadness behind a door locked by resentment. We bury our anger because we fear we will discover it is a rage burning out of control. Lack of control feels like chaos. Change is frightening. Rather than to risk all of this, we often choose to stick with what is familiar, even if it is very uncomfortable. One of the most familiar things in my life is anger. It is hard to let go of something—of anything—that you know very well.

When I was a child growing up in a dysfunctional home, my father had a monopoly on anger. He was the only one who was allowed to express it. His anger was almost always followed by violence, so anger became something to be feared. I avoided anger like the plague because I saw too well its horrible consequences.

Having been brought up poorly, some of us from dysfunctional homes have a lot to be angry about. Our anger has to go somewhere. It was not safe to express our anger openly and outwardly, so we went *inside* with it—where it fermented and aged and grew more potent—but never went away. It seeped out of us and into our environment like illegally dumped toxic waste—in the forms of depression (anger turned inward), substance abuse, poor grades, promiscuity, and juvenile delinquency. It seeped out in spurts of inappropriate rage and dreams of wild revenge.

When I entered recovery as an adult child from a dysfunctional family, I was encouraged to reclaim my rightful anger. It was suggested that the repression of my anger had turned it to rage, and that I should begin to express my anger so as to defuse the extreme volatility of that emotion. I came to believe that anger was a natural emotion which could actually help in some areas of my life—such as in setting boundaries—if I were to learn to deal with it appropriately. For example, if someone steals your new bicycle, anger is an appropriate response. You know your rights have been violated. You know you want back what is rightfully yours. And you know you want the person who violated your rights to be held responsible. But if you're an adult child from a dysfunctional family who looks at the ground, kicks the dust, and says to yourself, "Well, I really didn't deserve a new bicycle anyway," you're really setting yourself up for trouble.

This made a lot of sense to me. I had seen unexpressed anger in my life build up to an explosion which mortally wounded a few of my relationships. I did not want to repeat that. I had seen a close friend of mine, who had great difficulty expressing anger, develop high blood pressure, have a heart attack, and die. I did not want to be like him. I had seen how it was not possible to stuff just one emotion deep inside me. When I stuffed or numbed my anger, it meant that I tamped down everything else along with it—like joy, love, expectations. I want to change that.

So I allowed myself to get angry. It felt terrible at first. My cheeks shook. I broke out in a sweat. I developed a headache. I felt sinful expressing this "bad" emotion. My anger was quite unattractive, but it was necessary for me to finally accept that I had it.

I began to enjoy the expression of anger. Anger, sarcasm, and wit make a potent combination. The adrenaline that my anger released had a drug-like effect. My heart beat fast. My blood flowed quickly. My face was flushed and I felt warm. And best of all—I felt "right." I felt justified. Look at the way I was raised! Look at the way, as an adult, I had continued to allow people to treat me! No one could deny me the right to my anger! Anger became the fuel that propelled me through difficult situations. Anger became the passion that let me know I was alive!

I didn't *have* anger. I *was* anger. Anger was my first name. And blame was my middle name.

Then I realized that it was not getting angry but remaining angry that had become a problem for me. I saw how my anger alienated some people; then I got angry at those who could not deal with my anger. I got angry with myself for not being able to express anger at certain people who upset me. If someone hurt me, I would get angry instead of feeling the pain. It was difficult to let go of my attraction to blame and anger.

Gradually this attraction began to ebb, as I recognized that anger and hurt pride are the smoke screens behind which I hide some of my character defects. I try to remain angry at my parents. I try to work up a good head of steam. I want to wear my anger like a suit of armor to spare me from the pain. But I can't. I never had a childhood. Now I am losing my anger about never having had a childhood. What I am left with is...sadness. And facing sadness is not easy. All of my life I would rather have been dragged across a field of boulders by wild horses than to feel the immense sadness within me. Anger was so much easier to feel.

Now, finally, through forgiveness, some of these feelings have begun to change.

Blame

 I blame others for my shortcomings. I claim my parents made me the way I am. Therefore I can excuse my own abusiveness. My parents claim they should be excused for their abusive or neglectful behavior because they were drunk (or very busy or very nervous or very tired) at the time.

When an abusive parent blames a child as the reason for the abuse, the child believes it. Then the child grows up and learns to blame others. Around and around we go, and where we stop nobody knows. This blame-tossing perpetuates the dynamics of abuse which we were victims of as children, and which we continue to play out as adults.

I don't want to blame my parents for what is wrong with me. I am an adult and I want to take responsibility for my life. I don't want to get stuck in blame and anger at my parents. But part of accepting responsibility is to determine who is accountable for what. Since a lot of my character defects are the result of the way my parents raised me, holding my parents accountable for their part allows me to take responsibility for changing my life.

A huge obstacle in the path of accountability is denial. I deny how horrible my childhood was. I deny the lousy behavior of my parents. My most frequently used tactic of denial is to let my parents off the hook by saying things like, "They did the best they could." They did *not* do the best they could. They didn't even think about doing the best they could. But I have a need to believe they did.

Does anyone who gets drunk and beats his children sit down to wonder if he's parenting to the best of his ability? I doubt it.

Like other adult children from alcoholic and dysfunctional homes, I will go to any lengths to protect my parents, because I don't want to face the harsh fact that they were not there for me emotionally. I don't want to admit that my mother acted in utter disregard for my well-being.

I was treated with no respect by parents who had no respect for themselves. They had self-hate, and they taught self-hate to their children. I was neglected and abused. What they did to their children is immoral and illegal. They had problems of their own which caused them to act the way they did, but this rationale does not alter the fact that their neglect almost cost me my life. I nearly died at their hands. I nearly died at my own hands when, later in life, I played out the behavior and attitudes I had learned as a child.

The feelings of pain and loss and perpetual disappointment do not simply go away. They have remained lodged in me like a fish bone caught in my throat.

I am now allowing myself to feel the feelings I have never felt before. I must listen to the child within me that was ignored. And if one of the feelings that comes to the surface is blame, then I want to feel all there is to feel about blame. Then perhaps I can feel the anger behind the blame. And then the pain behind the anger. And the sadness behind the pain. And the acceptance that is rumored to lie behind the sadness. And the hope behind the acceptance. So that someday I may have a chance at leading a contented life.

The question no longer is: "Who is to blame?" or "How could they do such things?" The question is: "Who has been hurt and how can we get the survivors back on track?"

Forgiving Ourselves

Serenity does not come through confessing the sins of our parents. They are not the clay from which forgiveness is built. We, ourselves, are all we have to work with. If we are unforgiving of our parents, then we must surely be, on some level, unforgiving of others. And if we are unforgiving of others, then we must surely be, on some level, unforgiving of ourselves.

A good basis for our forgiveness of others is our forgiveness of ourselves. Forgiveness for what? Deep down, many of us believe we were responsible for the dysfunctions of our family. We believe that if we had only been better children then our parents would have been better parents.

For example, a father might say that age-old, famous line as he takes off his belt and prepares to whip his child, "This is going to hurt *me* more than it is going to hurt you." Then the child might say to himself, as he lies across his father's knee to receive the beating, "I'm sorry I'm hurting you, Daddy."

Later in life, when we were better able to emancipate ourselves emotionally from our parents, we might have felt justified at our negative feelings toward them. But by then we might have heard that our parents had a "disease" which made them act the way they did. Then we felt bad about blaming them for something that wasn't their fault.

How could we be so selfish? we asked ourselves.

It felt as if we were blaming someone for having cancer. So we began to talk ourselves out of our feelings thinking that we didn't deserve them. Maybe we weren't really so upset about our feelings after all, we told ourselves. Maybe it was something else that was bothering us.

I still carry these self-negating feelings into many of my daily affairs, although I am much quicker to realize when I am doing it. I remember when, a few years ago at Christmas time, my wife and I had just separated. I was the single parent of a two-year-old. I was living in a sublet apartment with the photographs of the primary tenant's happy family staring at me from the walls. I saw families getting into taxis with bundles of presents for loved ones. My birthday was coming up three days after Christmas. The sixth year anniversary of my having joined a recovery program was coming up on Christmas day. And my therapist informed me that she was leaving town for two weeks.

I became very upset when my therapist told me that. I told her that there should be a law that therapists could not leave their clients at holiday time. I asked her what she thought would happen if surgeons took holidays in the Carribean. I ranted and raved at her. And then she left anyway, leaving a number where she could be reached in an emergency.

I survived the two weeks without her, although the loneliness and isolation was crushing. It was several months before I was able to talk about the painful subject again. She eventually told me that she had left town because of a family emergency. She didn't want to go but she had to.

"Why didn't you tell me that in the first place?" I asked her, feeling selfish and naughty and not considerate of others' feelings.

"I didn't tell you because I didn't want you to talk yourself out of your feelings. I didn't want you to beat yourself up for feeling abandoned," she replied. "No matter what my reasons for leaving, you had a right to your feelings about being left."

That episode with my therapist helped me to reverse the tendency, which I had learned so well as a child, to think that I am wrong and selfish for having "negative" feelings. I came to believe that I must acknowledge that I have mixed feelings about my parents and every other significant person in my life. I saw that, as part of the process of forgiveness, I had to investigate the origins of this tendency to blame myself whenever something goes wrong with someone else.

Often we fail to realize that, in addition to the dysfunctions within ourselves, it is the dysfunctions in the family, resulting in a lack of nurturing, which do so much harm to our ability to have healthy relationships. Whether our parents' lack of nurturing is intentional or not—whether it is caused by chemical dependency, depression, physical ill-ness, death, workaholism, or anything else—we must realize that we have taken on some of the blame.

There are many things we might stop blaming—and consider forgiving—ourselves for:

- not being able to cure our parents (which we told ourselves any decent child should be able to do)
- not living up to our parents' expectations of us, and punishing ourselves for not doing so (my father wanted a lawyer; he got a poet)
- not being a perfect child
- making mistakes
- not being able to save our siblings (we told ourselves that if we cared enough we would have been able to do so)
- treating ourselves the way our parents treated us
- abandoning ourselves when the going gets tough (by shutting down emotionally)
- developing the same dysfunctions we deplored in our parents (such as chemical dependency, overeating, or poor parenting)

Ultimately, we have to forgive ourselves for being ourselves. Have you ever sat in your room, staring out through the window, feeling a little down, watching people walk by? Don't they look great? They are just chugging along, dressed so well, clean and fresh looking, on their way to their meaningful jobs, leading their meaningful lives. We imagine them with no holes in their socks, no blemishes under their make-up, no ghosts in their closets, no drunks in their families. We imagine them happy that it is Monday morning again, that now that they are well-rested from their weekends at the beach with their flawless lovers they can get back to being productive in their lucrative, high-visibility careers.

And what about us? If we break a shoelace, we can trace it back to being from a dysfunctional home. If we do anything less than perfectly, we are flawed human beings, the objects of self-pity and scorn. If we make a simple mistake, it is a relapse.

Many of us look out through our windows and think that those "normal" human beings know how to do "it" right and we don't. We put ourselves at a psychological disadvantage. We chastise our-selves for being confused or for not having "pure" motives (whatever *they* may be).

I called a friend the other day and confessed to him that I had been cunning, baffling, and manipula-tive with my daughter. I wanted her to have a play-date with her friend so I would be free to go to my health club and make a pass at my aerobics instruc-tor, whom I suddenly had a crush on. I knew that the parents of my daughter's friend were busy that day, but I encouraged my daughter to call them anyway, in hope that they "simply couldn't say no" to my sweet little girl. Well, they did say no, and there will not be a play-date and I will not be able to go to my aerobics class. Shucks! My attempts at manipulation failed again. I felt terrible for inflicting my character defect upon my daughter.

My friend said, "I can't see what you did wrong." I was shocked. He continued, saying, "Human beings are not pure. They have conflicting emotions and multiple motives. Sometimes I do someone a favor because I love that person *and* I want a favor in return *and* I am afraid of rejection. So what? That doesn't negate the fact that I am doing someone a favor."

I used to think that being perfect was being human. Anything less than that was shameful. I was raised in such a dysfunctional way that I have some pretty bizarre ideas of what it means to be human. Only a saint or a dead person is capable of not making a single false move. If I can forgive myself for simply being a human being, it will make this process of recovery much simpler and more enjoyable.

Sometimes I don't know what I'm doing and that's okay. I'm new at this. I've never walked the face of the earth as a human being before, at least not that I can remember, and sometimes I'm not very good at it. Sometimes I feel like an awkward little boy with two left shoes. That little boy is occasionally hard to accept. I would prefer to recover gracefully and in private. But my recovery seems to be happening in groups and with less than perfect posture and diction on my part. I am learning to accept myself even for the things I don't like about myself. I am open to all aspects of me—not like picking through cherries in a grocery store bin, where only the perfect ones are acceptable.

Ultimately we have to forgive ourselves for being human. To forgive our own humanity means we have to be understanding of our parents' humanity. We are not judges or executioners. Yet forgiveness would be unnecessary if we had not judged and condemned our parents in the first place. We are not the final authority on the rightness or wrongness of other people's behavior.

In order to forgive my parents, I must have already decided they are guilty of whatever I am about to forgive them for. That means I have placed myself in the position of knowing who is guilty and who is not. Then I decide who is to be punished or forgiven. I have adorned myself with a crown of resentments. I am the standard against which all goodness is measured. I am a self-appointed judge and executioner. I have relieved God of most of his duties.

I sit and wonder how I can forgive my parents without having judged them guilty. I can't. Guilty of what? Of having been ill? Of having been born into a bad family situation the same way I was? These are questions I must ask myself.

I cannot forgive my parents if I cannot forgive myself. The same executioner who screams, "Off with their heads!" every time I discover yet another way my parents abandoned me emotionally—that same executioner is out to get me every time I make a mistake. The executioner does not discrim-inate between me and others. The executioner wants blood—any blood. The only way for me to be spared is to declare an unconditional amnesty for all prisoners of the chaos of dysfunction. Then my parents and my friends and I and all the wounded, defensive people who suffer in silence and in fear of retribution can come out and talk about what happened and where to go from here.

I am raising the white flag of enlightened surrender. Getting back, or getting over, or getting even is not the name of the game. The name of the game is Learning to Love and Live. Let's get on with it.

We can learn to accept (but not necessarily like) our parents for who and what they are, instead of who and what we wish them to be. We are powerless over our parents' behavior. We are powerless over the way they view the past. We have only ourselves to forgive. We can forgive ourselves for being judgmental, for not having all the answers. If we don't forgive ourselves, that inability or unwillingness to do so can be just as harmful to us as whatever we're struggling to forgive our parents for.

We may never know why our parents behaved the way they did. Often it was the only way they knew how to behave. Our parents may never have harmed a single person intentionally in their lives. Their errors may have been more of omission—what they didn't do—than of commission—what they did do. With my father it was more what he *did do* which damaged his children. With my mother it was more what she *didn't* do which damaged us. Either way, the damage was done.

Detaching

My parents live several hundred miles away. I hear from them about three times a year. My father contacted me once when I'd been walking around for two days thinking about him. Meditating on forgiveness seemed to be working. I believe things come to me when I am ready to deal with them. Lately it has been as if a skywriter has etched on a blue Sunday afternoon celestial chalkboard the word "FORGIVE."

I sometimes think my father can catch wind of my softening and, as if by some odd, dysfunctional law of coincidence, as soon as my rage at him lessens—he appears with spurs on his heels, teeth filed to a point, cracking his knuckles, and smiling a provocative smile.

He tries to offend me until I push him away. It is as if he pours gasoline on my love for him and then asks me for a light. Then he becomes angry at my refusal, and tries to punish me for not play-ing along with him. Sometimes it seems that he hates himself for loving me. And when a feeling of love or even a morsel of compassion comes up in either one of us, he will get nasty or vulgar or sarcastic or use any one of his number of tools of long-distance abuse so that the Plexiglas wall of distrust will snap back up between us.

I am afraid that my father doesn't want to be forgiven. He doesn't want to forgive, either. I might call my father today and say to him, "Dad, I have been doing a lot of reading on forgiveness lately. Actually, I've written a small book on the subject. Once in a while I speak on the subject at these meetings I attend, which are aimed at healing people who suffered abuse during their childhoods. The subject of forgiveness has come up a lot with my therapist recently. I feel that now, after many years of reflection and prayer, I am ready to forgive you." I am afraid that his response probably would be, "Forgive me for what?"

My feeling is that my parents probably think more about TV dinners than they do about forgiveness. I really believe they think they did nothing wrong. They live in a glass bubble of denial. If the subject of the past ever comes up when I speak with my father, and it rarely does, he usually launches into a diatribe about the failed lives of his children. At the tail end of his monologue, he usually adds a single sentence declaring appreciation that I am in recovery from substance abuse.

The focus is always on me and what I am doing about my troubled life, never about him and what he is doing about his. Quite often I fall into the trap of listening to his expressions of concern, not realizing that they are less about looking at me than they are about *not* looking at him.

The problem is that forgiveness changes the dynamics of our relationship. My father is uncomfortable with that. So am I, to a lesser extent. Life sometimes seems easier in icy silence. They lead their lives. I lead mine. Once in a while we pretend to talk. We try to keep it clean and above the belt. Then we say goodnight and go back to the "peace and quiet" of our non-family relationship.

Forgiveness is difficult stuff. Finding everyone in the family ready and willing to participate is not easy. But I know that I need to forgive my parents for my own benefit, regardless of their ability to receive or give forgiveness.

Once we have begun to forgive ourselves—but before we can forgive our parents—we must learn to detach from the highly-charged emotional drama of our family. We can ease out of the role of the abused child who harbors resentment, keeps score, and plots revenge.

When we can step aside from this family craziness, forgiveness becomes possible because we can see more clearly the ways in which the members of our family relate to each other. By becoming detached enough to allow the family dynamics to come into focus, we gain perspective on our problems.

By continuing to focus on the harm our parents have done to us, beyond recognizing what happened and how we feel about it, we negate the responsibility we have to ourselves to undo the wreckage of the past. When we hold on to rage at our parents, we are still holding on to our parents.

When we let go of the rage, we let go of the grip we allow our parents to have on us.

There has been, perhaps, enough suffering all around. Our unforgiveness only keeps us plugged in to the family drama which offers infinite reruns of the story of neglect. When we cling to unforgiveness, the band plays on and on and on and we can't seem to get that melody out of our head. Unforgiveness perpetuates the suffering in us and does nothing to end it.

Not Forgiving

As I said early in this book, forgiveness is a choice. We have a right to consider some things unforgivable, such as sexual abuse or any form of repeated, malicious invasion of personal boundaries. There is no one, other than you, who has the right to judge your recovery in a negative light because of your inability or unwillingness to forgive a particular incident or episode.

But the lack of forgiveness may signal that something more is going on besides our rightful and understandable refusal to forget what has been done to us.

For example: We might use unforgiveness as a way of punishing our parents. Our conspicuous absence at special family occasions, not returning phone calls, our silence amidst laughter or our laughter amidst sadness—these are indirect ways of hurting them, of paying them back for what they did to us.

When we refuse to play the role expected of us in our dysfunctional home—things change. Our family may be very disappointed in us. They might resent us for getting better because they need us to keep the game going. They may feel abandoned. We might feel as if we are abandoning *them* to a lifetime of misery that only we can save them from, as if they may die without us.

In my own life—as I worked on forgiveness and witnessed the changes and developments in the family dynamics—I began to feel guilty. There are many family members I have left behind, who seem to be less fortunate than me. I felt guilty because I was getting out of the unhealthy situation in time to save myself. I felt somewhat unworthy of the health I have, which some other members of the family seem incapable of. I have a tendency, which I battle daily, to want to throw away my achievements so that I can grovel in the pain, where a small part of me thinks I still belong. It seems I suffer from survivor's guilt.

This is not a new feeling to me. Let me give you an example. I am the youngest of a large family. I remember as a small child being told that the last thing my parents needed or wanted, when they discovered my mother was pregnant with me, was another child. But they quickly added that, once they saw me and realized how wonderful I was, they fell in love with me and changed their minds.

When they told this to me, I was a crippled child. I was crippled with a hip disease, and I walked on crutches for five years between the years of two and seven. If they didn't want a child in the first place, imagine how they felt about having a crippled one? I really didn't mind being crippled. I got a lot of candy handed to me by ladies in the grocery store. Being crippled also spared me from most of the beatings my mother and my siblings received. Even my father couldn't bring himself to beat a crippled five-year-old boy. At least not very often.

But I evened the score for him. I felt so guilty that I had been spared, and I wanted so much to be a part of my brothers' and sister's lives that, when I grew up and left my father and my crutches behind me, I began to beat myself with negativity and sensory deprivation and poor health and booze and drugs. Out of loyalty to my father, and empathy with my siblings, I picked up the whip and used it mercilessly on myself.

There are several reasons, other than feeling guilty about our recovery, why we might be reluctant to forgive our parents.

By not forgiving our parents—or by not forgiving a bus driver or the guy on the next bicycle, for that matter—we allow ourselves to feel contempt, superiority, and righteousness. By denying forgiveness, we allow ourselves to feel power over other people. It might even feel good...for a while.

By not forgiving our parents we are better able to cling to our favorite defects of character. Lack of forgiveness fosters the growth of my most cherished and time-worn alibis. I remember in early recovery a clear (and usually unspoken) message to my girlfriends was, "I have this fear of intimacy which originated in the way I was raised by my dysfunctional parents, so please don't expect much of me in this relationship." I was covered. How could she blame me when I ran away and left her? I was an Adult Child from a Dysfunctional Family.

Not forgiving our parents means we don't have to support them. We can stay angry and distant. If we break down the wall and forgive—we might have to talk to them! They might want to know details of our lives. They might call on Sunday mornings. They might get old and need money or personal care. Keep the wall up and none of this will happen.

Many people I have talked to feel that forgiving their parents is like a stamp of approval on what their parents did. They don't want to give their parents an excuse to remain within their denial. They feel that forgiveness will allow their parents to say something like, "Well, if it doesn't bother my kid, then why should it bother me?" If our parents wish to tell themselves that what they did is okay, because now they are forgiven, there is nothing we can do to stop them. Accepting forgiveness is an admission of wrongdoing. Being forgiven isn't particularly easy either.

It seems our only practical choice in forgiving our parents is to keep the focus on ourselves— that is, if we truly want to get out of the dysfunctional family. *Because to forgive is to finally leave home.*

There are many convincing arguments for not forgiving our parents. At different points in our recovery, some will make more sense than others. "No" turns to "maybe" which turns to "yes" and back again. A year ago I could never have even conceived of writing this book. Times change. So do we.

For me, forgiving my parents began to make more sense when I realized that, ultimately, not forgiving them was sort of like punishing them by holding my breath. Yes, they became concerned. But I was the one who turned blue and passed out. How am I to benefit from not forgiving? What reward is there for holding on to the anger?

There was no doubt that I, as an abused child, was the victim and my parents were the abusers. But, over time, as an adult in recovery, I realized that by holding on to the pain—by refusing to let go of it—I had become the victim AND the abuser. I was a victim because I was abused—and I was an abuser because I insisted on remaining a victim.

We might not realize that by not forgiving we hurt ourselves as much, if not more, than we hurt our parents. Nonforgiveness is an acid that eats away at the shiny surface of love.

Letting Go

If a child is in a game of tug-of-war with a parent and the child lets go of his or her end of the rope, what happens? The game is over. So why don't we simply let go of our parents? Then this painful process of forgiveness—and books like this one—would be unnecessary.

Letting go is a difficult thing to do. The dynamics of a dysfunctional home keep us plugged in and holding on for dear life. Many of us have been trying for years to make a bad situation feel right. When someone even mentions the possibility of letting go, we begin to feel as if we are being asked to relax and prepare for takeoff when the cockpit door is open and we can see that a child is in the driver's seat of the plane. We have to learn to take the child out of the driver's seat and trust that our adult self is capable of getting us where we want to go.

Letting go is an integral part of forgiveness. We can begin by being willing to let go of our unforgiving stance. We can admit that the events and feelings of our childhood really happened. We can stop blaming *ourselves* for what is essentially a *family* problem. We can stop telling ourselves—as an excuse to avoid looking at the history of our relationship with our parents—that we're making mountains out of molehills. We can admit to ourselves that, try as we may, the past cannot be undone. We can let go of our hope for a better yesterday.

We can begin to look at our parents in human terms. As small children, adults seemed huge to us. Our parents loomed even larger than other adults because of the power they had over us. We looked up to them in more ways than one. We assumed they knew what they were doing. We accepted their belief in what is right and what is wrong. They were like gods to us. We sometimes saw the world more through their eyes than through our own.

Now we are grown up and can detach from our parents. We no longer need be dependent on them for survival or approval. They seem much smaller now, about the same size as most other human beings. Perhaps they are old and frail. Perhaps they are no longer living, and snapshots and memories are all that remain of them. No matter what our particular situation with our parents, we can decide to take back some of the power we handed to them as children. We can begin to have a more realistic view of them. From this perspective, fundamental change is much more possible.

Forgiveness breaks the pattern of abuse. It is a way of saying, "I won't play this game anymore." The spell our parents had over us is broken. The labyrinth of our parent-child relationship that we were lost in is now filled with sand and sealed shut, never to be visited again. Through forgiveness, we free ourselves from the curse of poisonous parenting.

We can let go of our expectation that our parents will respond to our work on forgiveness. We may get cooperation, or we may get nothing in return. Our parents may believe they did nothing wrong. Even if they admit to themselves they did something wrong, they may not be able to admit it to their children. They might not have enough insight or recovery to respond to our direct approach with anything other than hostility. It takes courage and trust for parents to recognize they have wronged their children, and our parents may be lacking in these strengths.

I feel sorry for my parents. They have no relationship to speak of with their children. Now the same is true for their grandchildren. By trying to avoid the pain of life, they also avoided the joy. There is nothing I can do to change them. Once again, I feel powerless to save someone I love. They have a right to their own lives, no matter how tragic I consider them to be. And that feeling of powerlessness is very upsetting as long as I fight it and refuse to accept that, just as I live autonomously, my parents, too, live autonomously. I am independent of them. They are independent of me.

We can begin, without harsh judgment, to accept our parents for who they are rather than who we want them to be. We can allow our parents to be themselves. We can focus less on the image and more on the reality of our parents. We can let go of our unrealistic expectations of them. We can stop resenting them because they didn't live up to our expectations of them, in the way we didn't live up to their expectations of us.

Then we can let go of our unrealistic expectations of ourselves. A tension I feel between my parents and me is often a manifestation of a tension I feel within me. I tend to lash out at others for what I see that I don't like about myself. We can detach from the image we have of ourselves, and allow a more realistic glimpse of who we are, along with a vision of who we want to be, to come into focus.

My recovery is progressing quite well. I feel as if I am becoming a whole person. Rarely do I open my mouth and spit out a Xerox copy of my father's words. Seldom do I make choices based upon what some imaginary, perfect parent would want me to do. No longer do I mimic the sickness of my family so as to maintain a sense of belonging.

I have learned how to take care of my body so that I am physically quite healthy. Three days a week I go to my gym. I limit my intake of sugar and caffeine. I do not use alcohol, nicotine, or other drugs. I have learned how to hold on to a job and not make my employer into a father figure with whom I can play my favorite adult games of reward and punishment. I have managed to move out of a part of the country where I was not happy to New York City, where I am creating a sense of home for the first time in my life.

I am making decisions and changes based upon me and my needs. It feels great. No matter how it turns out, I have the sensation that I am—finally—leading my life, rather than just acting it out.

Through living my life on a day-to-day basis I have gathered lots of evidence that forgiveness will benefit us. It will free us from bondage—to the past, to our parents, and to our own blame and resentment.

Closing the Wound

My father called and we had a short conversation. At the end of it he said, "I love you. But you don't believe that, do you?"

"Yeah, I believe it," I muttered in a voice thick with hollow sentiment. When he hung up the phone I realized I had heard him say that to me many, many times. But I had never allowed myself to hear the deep sorrow and desperate plea for understanding that laced his strained words. I wanted more from him. I wanted him to come out and confess his crime, to admit to me that he had almost ruined the lives of his children. But no such confession was forthcoming. I wanted him to ask for *my* forgiveness of what he had done.

My father was telling me, in his own way, that he knew his behavior had cost him the love of his children. Perhaps the loss of the love of your children is punishment enough. My father has paid dearly for his actions. Whether he admits verbally to his mistakes or not will not alter the fact that the price of his negligence has been high. He is a sad, guilt-laden, lonely, isolated man who is cut off from his family, his feelings, and his God.

My parents are ghosts who live rent-free in my head. When I reach out to touch them, my fingers pass right through them as if I were trying to hold on to a cloud.

My parents didn't do a very good job. But I can forgive them anyway. I know that what is done is done. I feel bad for them. I am sorry that they have to live out their lives with children who either don't speak to them or who merely pretend to. Yes, my parents did not do the best they could, but I believe they did the only thing they could, which was to act out the abuse they learned when they were children. My parents, you see, were victims of family abuse just as I was.

Like waves lapping at a shore, generations of family abuse follow one another. There is a pattern, a method to the madness, which is made more difficult by the fact that the abuse doesn't always happen at a conscious level. My task is to bring it to a conscious level—to think about it and to talk about it and to feel the abuse now the way I never allowed myself to feel it as a child.

I do this because I fear that if I don't bring these issues out in the open, I will continue to act out from a base of revenge and rage and then it will be very hard, if not impossible, to break the pattern of family abuse.

By not dealing with the issues of my childhood, I kept myself trapped in resentment and I was unable to let go of my past.

Walking around angry at my parents squanders my precious energy, confuses my emotions, and depletes my physical health.

To forgive is to clear a space for change to occur. Plants need to be pruned so that light can filter through the remaining leaves and reach the soil where new life is struggling to grow. My past is like those dead leaves. I can keep watering and watering them, but they will not spring to life.

Forgiveness does not happen by reading a book, or by doing any *one* thing. Any wound, any rip in the fabric of a relationship, takes time to heal. And it takes work. Festering wounds need to be opened and drained, cleaned out, and exposed to fresh air and light.

Fear and desire are our compass points on this journey toward forgiveness: fear of painful memories as well as fear of being wounded again; and desire—desire to come to terms with our parents and with ourselves.

I still have hope that a mending of my relationship with my parents is possible. But there is so much history, I am not sure if we can have a future together. My parents are softening as they get older. I feel that this might make them more open to the possibility of mutual forgiveness. But they are also, with age, getting further and further away from the days when most of the abuse took place. They are old and tired and might not care to deal with this potent stuff.

Despite my parents' ability or inability to respond to my attempts at forgiveness, I have moved much closer to a resolution, a healing of the wound in our relationship. I have learned to accept that the journey toward forgiveness begins in pain. And I have been able to see that these uncomfortable feelings do not last forever. Time—and work—can heal this wound.

Tools of Forgiveness

There are several tools available to help us in the process of forgiving our parents.

To avoid the fear that by beginning to forgive our parents we will be opening the floodgates of abuse which once victimized us, we can set up a few rules which make us feel safer. We can begin to set up boundaries, which show us where our rights begin and where another person's end. These boundaries are flexible and can bend to accommodate change in our relationship with our parents. The object is to be open to change without letting others violate our sense of self and safety. We can choose our own rules.

Here are some hypothetical rules:

- Please do not call me before 8 A.M. or after 10 P.M.

- Let's not borrow money from each other.

- Don't criticize the person I am dating or am married to—or the way I am bringing up a child.

- Both of us have the right to refuse invitations without being criticized.

We can also begin to take back the power which we handed over to our parents. There are several reasons why children give over all their power to their parents, starting with the fact that this is demanded of them. In a dysfunctional home, this demand may begin with the parents' belief that by having a baby they will become complete, that then they will be understood and completely loved and accepted. But children are awkward packages. In order for them to fill their parents' emptiness, they must fall strictly under parental power and control. The child's mission is to become exactly what the parent wants and expects, regardless of what the child may want. This way parents can live vicariously through their children, meeting their own needs by proxy.

Children know instinctively that, in order to survive, they must remain in their parents' good favor. Seeking love and loving in return, they surrender power to their parents, as required by the dysfunctional laws of poor parenting. And the parents, unnurtured and incomplete, do nothing to encourage their children to become emotionally emancipated. This is unhealthy—and infuriating! But now we know better. Armed with insight and knowledge into the dynamics of our crazy families, we may find that those we do not forgive maintain their power over us. This need be true no longer.

No more must the mere sight or thought of our parents be enough to trigger resentment, fear, worry, or tears. Instead of seeking validation from them, we can validate *ourselves* or go to someone with whom we have a more trusting relationship.

By keeping our power based within ourselves, we see that our parents no longer have the influence over us they once did.

We can encourage ourselves and our children to talk about our feelings as they come up. Then there won't be as much need to forgive. If, as a result of open expression, our children are less prone to biting their tongues and harboring resentments, then grudges and hurt feelings will be less likely to accumulate. Willingness to discuss matters when they happen—instead of waiting for the "perfect moment" to bring them up—means they are not as subject to the distortion of memory, which plays the painful episode over and over again, until we lose perspective and problems loom larger than they are.

We can write a list of all the things we resent about our parents. Our feelings often seem to be in one big blob, and writing them down helps us to clarify and separate our problems. It's interesting to note how many items on that list are things we resent about ourselves. We are thus better able to see if some of the problems we attribute to our parents really have nothing to do with them. We can also see if we are blaming *ourselves* for any problems which really are a result of the way we were raised.

We can make a searching and honest inventory of our own attitudes. By listing our character defects and assets, as we see them, we can better assess what there is to forgive our parents for, as well as what our role in the strained relationship has been. When we begin to take inventory of ourselves, we should remember that adult children from dysfunctional homes tend to be very hard on themselves. A shopkeeper who takes inventory to see what's worth keeping and what's not doesn't hurl the merchandise to the floor and start screaming, "Look at this worthless junk that's been lying around all these years!" We need to be as accepting of ourselves as possible, realizing that any inventory will turn up stuff that is no longer useful.

Making an inventory and immediately launching into a negative self-description ("manipulative, selfish, dishonest, insincere...") is just another way of blaming ourselves the way we may have been blamed as children. It might be helpful to remember that some of these "character defects" were extremely useful for us, as children in a dysfunctional home, in order to defend ourselves against annihilation. A false sense of control, for example, helped me as a child to believe that I could keep chaos from destroying my family. Of course, now that I am an adult not living with my family of origin, I no longer need some of these ingrained character traits. An honest inventory of myself helps me unload the outmoded goods.

We can write a letter to our parents, whether they are living or not, telling them all the feelings we have about our relationship with them. We can make a vow to ourselves before we begin the letter that, no matter what we write, we need not mail the letter or show it to anyone else. This allows us to be more open and honest in the expression of our feelings because there will not be anyone there to criticize or judge them.

We can find someone who is a neutral party, such as a therapist, a member of the clergy, or a sponsor in a Twelve Step program, to talk to. A person with little involvement in our life may be able to respond with what is best for us.

Not all siblings in dysfunctional families have the same experiences, so a sibling or another member of the family may be able to provide us with a different side of the story. This can be helpful, if we keep in mind that their version might be as biased as ours. We can avoid looking for the "right" answer and accept all comments as helpful pieces of the puzzle.

While we are working on forgiving our parents, we can set aside ten minutes at the end of each day to review what has happened and how we feel about it. We might uncover some slights which our parents, or someone else, made against us which we tried to ignore or minimize.

We can, if we are so inclined, pray for our parents. This helps to release us from the bondage of resentment. Our parents have their own Higher Power, which some people choose to call God. We can, in our prayers, release our parents to the loving care of *their* Higher Power. Thus we are free of responsibility for their lives, and are better able to be responsible for our own. We might pray that, despite our past, we have the strength and courage and willingness to forgive and to be forgiven.

A fresh start is begun by the forgiveness of a false start. Unencumbered by the past, we are free to build a new future. We are able to break certain destructive patterns of behavior which our parents were unable to break. We find we are able to make mistakes. And people are not so afraid to make mistakes around us. We are more flexible because we have become able to forgive. We don't need to be overly critical or judgmental of others in order to justify our lack of forgiveness.

As we begin to forgive our parents, we begin to forgive ourselves. And we begin to forgive the world for not being perfect either.

Forgiveness and Children

As we learn to be forgiving of ourselves and of each other we learn to be forgiving of our children. We need not pass on to future generations what was passed on to us. A cold heart is hereditary. Love and acceptance are contagious.

My seven-year-old daughter, Celeste, is healthy. The miracle of miracles is that, considering what my childhood was like, I have been able to be a successful single parent even though I learned very few healthy rules about bringing up children.

I was getting my daughter ready for school the other morning and she said to me, "Were your parents mean to you?"

"Yes. They were." I replied, surprised at this question which came, apparently, out of nowhere.

"Why?" she asked.

"Uh...I'm not sure...I...uh...think they were mean because that is the way they were treated by *their* parents when *they* were little."

"Then it's really not their fault, is it?"

"No. I guess it isn't," I replied.

That was the end of the issue as far my daughter was concerned. Something bad had happened, but no one was to blame. It was like no-fault insurance. She was ready to forego the blame and focus on the repairs.

It is not that my daughter has no feelings about abuse. I know, for example, that when she sees a child being physically or verbally abused on a bus, she feels sorry for the child, is upset by what she sees, and feels powerless to intervene on behalf of the child. She knows that her father's childhood was like that. But she is not fixated on negative attitudes, the way her father sometimes still is. She looks at the abuse, sees if there is anything redeeming about the people involved despite the abuse, and then moves on.

Healthy children are eager to forgive. Last week my daughter and I were at a birthday party for a little girl. There were a lot of children there, perhaps too many. There were also a lot of four-letter words there (boys) so the party got a bit rowdy. The parents who were there discussed the wildness going on and we decided it was okay for the kids to act like kids at a party.

But one little girl, in all the excitement, popped the birthday girl in the nose. The hostess became very upset, called the child's mother, and told her she would have to come and pick up her daughter. The punishment the hostess decided upon was to not allow the "boxer" to attend the sleep-over which all the little girls had been invited to.

While the mother was on her way over to the birthday party to pick up her daughter, lots of kisses, hugs, and an ice pack were bestowed upon the birthday girl. It is a terrible thing to get slugged in the face on your birthday but, somehow, by the time the mother arrived, the birthday girl and her friends were begging the hostess to allow the "boxer" to stay for the sleep-over. This possibility was discussed between the two mothers. One mother said that a decision had been reached and they would have to abide by it or it would confuse the children. The other mother was embarrassed and defensive about her daughter's behavior. The responses of both mothers were perfectly understandable. The result, however, was that the child had to leave the party.

There is rarely, if ever, a clear "right" side and "wrong" side in these situations. And that is not the issue here. What I find interesting is that both mothers, like me, were raised in dysfunctional homes. Both felt threatened by this "act of violence." Both felt the need to do something in order to fix it. Neither parent looked at how unlikely it is that only one child had caused the episode, and how the birthday girl might have provoked the "boxer." Both failed to take into account that children in their innocence can sometimes be vicious. Both parents were, perhaps, reacting to the pain of similar situations in their own childhoods, which they projected onto their children—and then tried to save them from.

My point in these two stories—the one about my daughter telling me, while I was getting her dressed, that she didn't blame my parents for the way they raised me, and the other story about the scuffle at the birthday party—is that children raised in nurturing homes are willing and eager to forgive. Such children find it easier to forgive because they have love, respect, and acceptance—tools necessary for forgiveness.

Healthy children seem to believe that people are basically good. And part of that basic goodness in people is the freedom to get angry, to make a mistake by offending or abusing someone, to feel sorry for doing so, to make amends as best you know how, and to get back to the party.

Healthy children have a lot of answers. I am sometimes jealous that they instinctively know how to deal with many of their problems. Children left alone will often figure out a solution to their own conflicts. I have learned something about negotiating for my own needs by listening to children create and then agree on rules governing their own behavior.

It is we adults raised in dysfunctional homes who have to learn that whisking a child out of conflict by taking her home to be alone is not necessarily the best way to help her learn to deal with others. We adults, whom our children sometimes observe as we act like retaliators and blame-seekers, are the carriers of dysfunction from one generation to the next. We teach what we know. Now we can learn new ways of dealing with old problems.

I believe that forgiveness is a natural function of a healthy spirit. Children can be great teachers. We stand to learn a lot from the deep-seated, open-ended spiral of forgiveness growing ever upward in the spirit of a well-loved, well-nurtured child.

The day after the birthday party where the hitting took place, my daughter and I sat at the breakfast table where we often discuss things from the previous day which we feel were unresolved. I asked her about her feelings toward forgiveness.

"Could you forgive someone," I asked her, "who got on the bus and shook an umbrella all over your brand-new school clothes and then walked away whistling, like nothing was wrong?"

"Yes," she said adamantly, "because they didn't know they were doing it." My daughter is a little better than I am about presuming the perpetrator innocent until proven guilty. She assumed the person meant no harm. She appears to have a basically positive attitude toward people.

"I have another question for you, Celeste," I said. Celeste licked her lips. She savors being included in what sounds like an adult conversation almost as much as she enjoys ice cream. She wiggled around in her seat to get comfortable just the way people do who are being interviewed on Sunday afternoon television quiz shows.

"What if someone," I continued, "got on the bus and stepped on your foot and knew they did it but kept on walking and didn't say anything. Could you forgive *that* person?"

"No," she snapped, and then paused a moment and said, "Yes. I mean, maybe." She thought further. "I could forgive them but it would be hard. Maybe I wouldn't want to forgive them. Are you supposed to?"

"It depends," I said, admitting to myself that my answer was a cop-out, but, more importantly, not wanting to take the focus off her feelings as she scanned me for clues to the "right" answer.

"What if the person who stepped on your feet said 'I'm sorry'?" I asked.

"I would forgive him," Celeste said with confidence and finality.

It seemed that, central to my daughter's ability and willingness to forgive, is a desire for the person she is trying to forgive to make an apology or to assume at least some responsibility for his or her part in the problem.

Adults have the option to pull away from or leave an abusive relationship. Children are not always able to drop out of school or run away from home, so they avoid the abuse as best they can. Children often run within.

That is what happened to me as a child. I ran inside. I pulled my isolation over me like a blanket. I snuggled up against the warm fire of my anger. I treated my resentment like a pet—stroking it, talking to it, feeding it. My hurt turned to anger. My willingness to forgive became a difficulty with forgiveness which turned into a refusal to forgive. Brick by brick, I built a fortress around me until it was complete and I felt safe. But I forgot to build a door. No one could get in, which was the way I had planned it. But I couldn't get out, which was more than I had bargained for. I don't want to live in a fortress. I want to live in a home. Forgiveness is the door leading out of a cold, enclosed heart.

My daughter has an imperfect father. I'm sure I'm committing acts that I don't even recognize which my daughter will grow up and try to forgive me for. I'm doing the best I can, but that is no guarantee that Celeste will not have to work through some unhealthy parenting practice I unknowingly employ. I don't want to cause my precious little daughter any pain, but I know it will, to some degree or other, happen.

I don't want to cause myself any unnecessary pain either, but I know that it is my own unresolved issues that I see surfacing in my child which hurt the most. Issues of pain and forgiveness arise between children. They arise between adults. They most certainly arise between children and adults. It happens in all families, not just dysfunctional ones. Children and adults alike are hurt in a gridlock of anger and stubborn unforgiveness.

I have met people in recovery who are afraid to have children for fear that they will ruin their lives. I also see many, many people in recovery who are learning how to have intimate relationships *despite* the way they were raised. These people are learning how to love. That very love is the sustenance of our future generations. I have hope that, because of the work I am doing in recovery, the closest my daughter will ever come to the kind of abuse I knew will be to read a book about it.

The day may come when my daughter will not be able to identify emotionally with some of the relationship issues which her father has. It has already happened to an extent. Fear of intimacy, shame, terminal shyness, stuffing feelings—these are absent in her character. I have seen my seven-year-old daughter scratch her head in loving puzzlement about what life must be like with so much fear. She is a different person than I am. She can't relate to being raised in a dysfunctional home. Amazing.

Out of Chaos

I am a man with troubles. I live day to day with monsters in my head. I am sometimes confused and weary. I feel, whether it is true or not, that I have to work harder at life than most people do. A plague, like alcoholism or any family dysfunction, will snake its way through a population, leaving in its wake a mass of people wandering around sick, tired, and confused. And, as if that isn't bad enough, they strain their brains trying to figure out what they did to deserve such a fate.

"I DID NOTHING WRONG! WHY ME?" I shouted heavenward. "WHY NOT YOU?" was the heavenly answer.

That made sense to me. Perhaps I was hit, and hit hard, by this plague because my Higher Power knew that I was strong enough to take it, to live through it, and to talk about it with my daughter, with you, and eventually with my parents.

Actually, I have been more than spared. My experience has sharpened my vision. Out of chaos my parents crafted a strong and talented man. Without the tragedy I have suffered, I would not have been motivated to get to know myself as well as I have. I might have died a stranger to myself. I might have died before I lived. How ironic that partly because of how bad it was in the past I can appreciate how good it is today.

The chaos was not my fault. Craziness and disease are not moral issues. They are physical, mental, and spiritual issues. So I do not blame myself for what happened in my crazy life. Nor do I accept blame that others might try to put on me. It is hard to accept, when things go as wrong as they did in my life, that there are no villains, only victims. Even the perpetrators are victims.

My parents have led long and difficult lives. My life of hell ended when I entered recovery at the age of twenty-nine. My parents' lives are a standard against which I can measure my growth—that shows me I have come a long, long way to where I am today. They are in their seventies and quite ill. The range of their emotions is narrow—from pain to numbness. They are not evil. They are sad and troubled, doing the best they can with the limited tools of living they possess. I want to rewrite their lives. I want to open my chest and hand them my heart. I am strong. My heart can beat for the three of us. But here I am slipping into my fantasy world again!

I can only save myself. I can build a life worth living to the best of my ability. I can look to my parents and learn from their mistakes. I can be grateful that I can see the pitfalls they encountered and avoid some of them for myself. I am very sorry that, for reasons I will probably never know, my parents never found recovery. But I did. I have been spared.

Because of my newfound ability and willingness to forgive, I appreciate that my having been raised in chaos has given me a new vision of heaven and earth. Because I was brought up in a dysfunctional home, I have found myself on a spiritual journey that I never otherwise would have ventured on. There have been many rewards. Out of chaos came order. Out of madness came a path to sane living. Out of apathy and defeatist thinking came a new resolve to turn my life around. Out of blindness came insight. Out of scorched hands reaching for love came forgiveness.

Recovery is an ongoing process that takes time and commitment. It does not happen all at once. Forgiveness has no end point. We never arrive at "it." We are always on the way there, getting closer all the time. Forgiveness is more a journey than a destination. During this journey, situations come up that require us to rethink and rework feelings and actions we thought had been resolved. We might find ourselves forgiving a person we have already once forgiven. We might find that person forgiving us—perhaps for the same thing we had so much trouble forgiving him or her for. Forgiveness gets easier with time and experience. The pain is not as intense, nor does it last as long. Once we find we are *able* to forgive, we have the choice of deciding whom to forgive, and when, and for what reason.

Some of us approach forgiveness like honor-student chemists, trying to mix the right amount of meetings, literature, treatment centers, therapy, relationships, subliminal tapes, brown rice, and aerobics to find the way out of our discomfort. We forgive and forgive until we are exhausted. We can't understand why not much has happened when we have tried everything!

Then perhaps we try nothing. For, above all, forgiveness is a gift of grace. Caught between a shattered past and an unforgiving heart—we find it a miracle any of us get out of dysfunctional family systems at all. Caught between an unchangeable past and a fear of change in the present—we find it a miracle that any of us have anything to look forward to except more of the same pain we have already been through.

Yet somehow, through grace, we are transformed. Despite what we think we are doing "right" and what we know we are doing "wrong," we have become reconciled—to our parents perhaps, but, more importantly, to ourselves.

> Grant me the serenity
> to accept the parents
> I cannot change,
> courage to change
> my destructive attitudes,
> and the wisdom
> to envision the rewards
> of doing so.

Forgiveness is a manifestation of spiritual evolution. It is an act of love and acceptance. It is an admission of our own ability to err, and of our need to be forgiven. We forgive so that we may be forgiven. We accept others so that we may be accepted by others and by ourselves. We *can* ask for forgiveness from each other.

By acknowledging and forgiving the limitations and excesses of others, we acknowledge and forgive the limitations and excesses of ourselves.

Then we are free to take responsibility for ourselves, to get out from under the shadow of our parents, to let go of our end of the tightrope of abuse, and to get on with the rest of our lives.

Epilogue

I have looked back, but I did not stare. There is no future there. Looking back has not killed me as I once feared it would. My past did not swallow me up like a huge wave and tumble me to pieces. No, looking back did not kill me, but it didn't save me either. Looking back has given me insight into the solution, but it is not the solution itself. I am ready to go on.

With this insight, knowledge, and grace, I will share my recovery with anyone who wants it. Recovery is contagious. Many symptoms of having been poorly parented have been stripped away. Many signs of recovery have taken their place.

I do not regret my past. I am not ashamed of it. I am a proud and healthy man. I am the son of parents and I am the parent of my daughter. We all share the same blood. Although I would write my life story differently if I had the chance, I can accept it now. I no longer want to sew a gold thread around the edges of denial.

I carry my recovery like a precious gift that has been placed in my hands, knowing that if I drop it, it will break. The gift is life today. It has taken every single day of my existence to get me to this moment. And at this moment I feel alive and well and hopeful. Mine is a life worth living, a life worth waiting for!

Most of my life has been a long drought. But now, partially because of the process of forgiveness, my family tree is blossoming again. Buds appear on bare branches. Without my parents, this journey of recovery would not have been possible.

About the Author

Dwight Lee Wolter, author of the acclaimed *A Life Worth Waiting For!* (also from CompCare Publishers) for adult children of alcoholism and other family dysfunctions, lives in New York City with his young daughter, Celeste. He is a poet, journalist, lecturer, and performance artist with a special interest in the issues of single parents, and of adults who grew up in families affected by substance abuse and other dysfunctions. In Wisconsin he was a member of the Governor's Council on Children and Youth, a member of the Poetry in the Schools program, and a state champion original orator. He is co-founder of Quest Publishing and editor and publisher of Nobody Press.

What book reviewers and human service professionals have said about Dwight Lee Wolter's *A Life Worth Waiting For!*

(also see page 92):

"Not a 'how-to' for adult children of alcoholics.... It is, rather, one man's triumphant proclamation of freedom—freedom from addictions, from self-pity and all the destructive emotions and patterns of behavior that have dogged him and most adult children of alcoholics since childhood. A rough and liberating read for anyone who has ever had anything to do with alcoholism."

Margaret E. Guthrie, the *Capital Times*, Madison, Wisconsin

"Dwight Lee Wolter...finds a new life, free of 'past ghosts and present insecurities'.... That means penetrating layers of denial to what really happened, facing it, releasing it, and then moving beyond all the pain to understanding."

Sue Miller in the *Los Angeles Times*

"Sometimes rawly emotional, sometimes funny, sometimes soaring with joy and exuberance, Wolter is at once wise and searching, teacher and child...."

Liz Mitchell, *Today's Chicago Woman*

"Heart-rending, almost painfully eloquent in its honesty, Dwight Lee Wolter's *A Life Worth Waiting For!* is a triumph of the human spirit. Pick up the best novel you can find, and read this book instead!"

> F. Forrester Church, Ph.D., minister,
> Unitarian Church of All Souls, New York;
> *New York Post* columnist;
> author of *Everyday Miracles:*
> *Stories from Life.*

"Dwight Lee Wolter vividly and powerfully describes growing up in a dysfunctional family. More significantly, he shares the processes, feelings, and rewards of recovery. His story is a moving book that touches the deep pain—and the possible joy —shared by adult children of alcoholics."

> Sharon Wegscheider-Cruse, author, lecturer;
> president, Onsite Training and Consulting;
> founding board chairperson, National
> Association of Children of Alcoholics
> (NACoA)

"Extremely moving. It made me laugh and then cry.... I enthusiastically endorse his work."

> John Bradshaw, author,
> *Bradshaw On: The Family* and
> *Healing the Shame that Binds You*

Dwight Lee Wolter's *A Life Worth Waiting For!* (CompCare Publishers) is available in bookstores. Or use this form to order *A Life Worth Waiting For!* directly from the publisher.

A Life Worth Waiting For!
For all Adult Children of Alcoholics
Messages from a Survivor
Dwight Lee Wolter
Trade paperback, 260 pages
Catalog number B00380

Quantity	Unit price	Total
_____	$10.95	_____

Postage/Handling Charges	
Amount of Order	Charge
up to $10.00	$2.00
$10.01 to $25.00	$3.00
$25.01 to $50.00	$3.50
$50.01 to $75.00	$5.00

Postage/Handling _____

Your State Sales Tax _____

GRAND TOTAL _____

☐ Check enclosed, payable to CompCare Publishers.

Charge my credit card: ☐ Visa   ☐ Mastercard

Acct. No. _____ Exp. _____

Name _____

Street _____

City_____ State _____ Zip _____

Order by mail using the form above. Send to: CompCare Publishers, 2415 Annapolis Lane, Minneapolis, MN 55441

For fastest service order by phone (charge orders only please). Call toll free 1-800-328-3330. In Minnesota, call 612-559-4800 collect.

Price subject to change.